CREATING CREATURE CRAFTS

CREEPY-CRAWLY CRAFTS

ANNALEES LIM

WINDMILL
BOOKS
New York

CONTENTS

Welcome to the world of creepy-crawlies!

Are bugs your favorite animals? Would you like to make some of your own and find out loads of fun facts about them along the way? Then this book is for you! Follow the step-by-step instructions on each page to craft termites, dragonflies, spiders and much more.

A lot of the projects use paint and glue. Always cover surfaces with a piece of plastic or layers of old newspaper. Whenever you can, let the project dry before moving on to the next step. This keeps things from getting stuck to each other and paint from smudging.

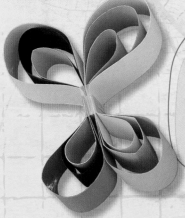

A note about measurements

Measurements are given in U.S. form with metric in parentheses. The metric conversion is rounded to make it easier to measure.

So, do you have your craft tools at the ready? Then get set to make your creepy-crawlies and discover what makes each of them so special!

3

SPARKLY LADYBUG

You will need:
- Egg carton
- White glue, paintbrush
- Red glitter
- Black sequins
- Black card stock
- Scissors
- Pencil
- Ruler
- Compass
- Glue stick
- Googly eyes

Ladybugs have brightly colored, hard wing cases that protect their folded wings. This ladybug's wing cases are covered in glitter so they shimmer and sparkle!

1

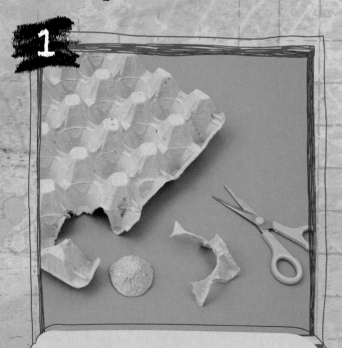

Use the scissors to cut out an egg carton section. It should be about 1½ inches (4cm) high.

2

Cover the egg carton section in glue and sprinkle red glitter all over it. Leave to dry.

3

Use a compass to measure a circle of black card stock that is a bit bigger than the base of the egg carton section. It should be about 2 inches (5cm) wide. Cut this out.

4

Cut out 2 thin strips of black card stock that are 1½ inches (4cm) long. Stick these onto the black circle and curl the ends using your pencil.

5

Stick your egg carton section onto the black circle using the glue. Use the glue to attach the black sequins that make the ladybug spots. Glue on the googly eyes.

LADYBUG FACT
The bright color and spots on a ladybug's wing cases are a warning to birds: they tell birds that they shouldn't eat this animal because it tastes nasty.

SNAIL STAMP

Did you know that no two snail shells are the same? Create your own unique snails with this crafty shell stamp!

You will need:
Thick cardboard, 4 by 4 inches (10 x 10cm)
White glue
Ball of string
Paint and paintbrush
Light blue card stock, 8½ by 11 inches (21.5 x 28cm)
Green paper, 8½ by 11 inches (21.5 x 28cm)
Colored paper
White paper
Scissors
Glue stick
Adhesive tape
Googly eyes
Tape measure

1

Cut 3 lengths of string that are each 20 inches (50cm) long. Use some tape to join them together at one end. Braid the strings and use tape to join their ends together.

2

Tape the braid to the middle of the card square. Carefully cover the rest of the cardboard with a layer of glue.

3

Stick the string onto the cardboard in a spiral shape. Make sure you keep the string as flat as possible. Leave this stamp to dry before using it in Step 5.

4

Cut out a grass border from green paper and some snail body shapes from colored paper. Glue all the pieces onto the light blue card stock. Add googly eyes.

5

Cover the stamp with paint. Place it on white paper and press down firmly. Lift off the stamp to reveal your print. Cut out the print and glue it to a snail body.

SNAIL FACT
Snails can seal themselves into their shells and stay there for months! They do this if the weather is too hot and dry for them.

SPIDERS IN A WEB

Spiders create webs to catch food. Weave your very own sparkly spider's web and craft some googly-eyed spiders, too!

1

Scrunch up 2 large pieces of tissue paper into a ball. Do the same with a small piece of tissue paper. Glue both balls together to make the spider body and head.

2

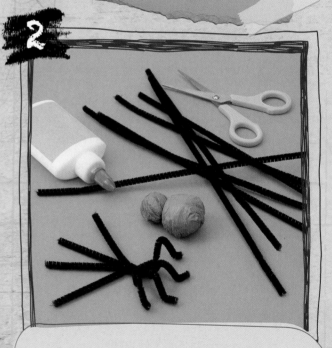

Cut 2 pipe cleaners in half and twist all 4 pieces together. Bend the ends of the pipe cleaners into leg shapes and glue them to the body.

3

Repeat steps 1 and 2 with different colored tissue paper. Stick googly eyes on each spider.

4

Starting in the middle of the purple card stock, sew a star shape into the card stock using the silver embroidery thread. Ask an adult to help you.

5

Start in the center of the star you have stitched and use the embroidery thread to weave a coil shape onto it. Place your spiders on their web!

SPIDER FACT
The silk that spiders make to weave their webs is finer than our hair, but it is stronger than steel!

BUTTERFLY PAPER CHAIN

Butterflies have four brightly colored wings. Create a chain of butterflies with colorful wings to decorate your room!

1

Cut 3 paper strips so that one is 8 inches (20cm) long, one is 6¼ inches (16cm) long and one is 4¾ inches (12cm) long. Staple them all together at one end.

2

Bend the paper strips so that the ends all line up, without making a crease in the paper. Staple them together. Repeat steps 1 and 2.

3

Make 2 smaller shapes in the same way as in steps 1 and 2, but use strips that are 6 inches (15cm), 4⅜ inches (11cm), and 3½ inches (9cm) long.

4

Use tape to join all the paper shapes to make a butterfly.

5

Make as many butterflies as you want in the chain. Join them all together by stapling the top wings to each other. Tie a piece of ribbon to each end of the chain to hang it up.

BUTTERFLY FACT

Did you know that butterflies taste with their feet? Their sense of taste is 200 times stronger than ours!

SHINY DRAGONFLY

Dragonflies are some of the fastest fliers in the insect world! Craft yours with wings that shimmer and glisten in the Sun.

You will need:
Flat kitchen sponges
Metallic paint
Gold paint
Scissors
White glue
Paintbrush
Wooden clothespin
Thin black marker

1

Paint 2 sponges with a layer of metallic paint. Remember to leave the sponges to dry before painting the other side.

2

Paint the clothespin gold and leave to dry.

3

Cut out 4 long, thin ovals for the wings, a long, thin shape for the body, and a circle for the head. Cut out 5 small rectangles.

4

Use a marker to draw the veins of the wings onto each oval.

5

Glue the head and body onto the clothespin, and decorate with small rectangles. Glue the wings onto the body and leave your dragonfly upside down to dry.

DRAGONFLY FACT

Did you know that dragonflies catch their food with their feet? They only eat prey that they have caught in flight.

JEWEL BUG

Jewel bugs are some of the most colorful insects in the world! Use this fun sgraffito (scratching) method to make your own gem-like creepy-crawlies.

You will need:
2 sheets of white card stock, 8½ by 11 inches (21.5 x 28cm)
Green paper
Blue, green, red and black crayons
Toothpick
Scissors
Green felt-tipped pen
Glue stick
Black marker

1

Color white card stock with blue, green and red crayons.

2

Cover all of your crayon markings with black crayon.

3

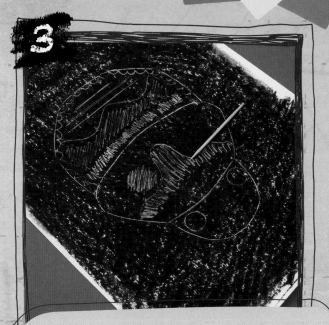

Use a toothpick to scratch off the black crayon layer in the shape of a bug body and head. Cut your bug out. Scratch off patterns, too.

4

Cut out leaf shapes from green paper. Use a green felt-tipped pen to draw leaf veins onto them. Glue the leaves to a piece of white card stock.

5

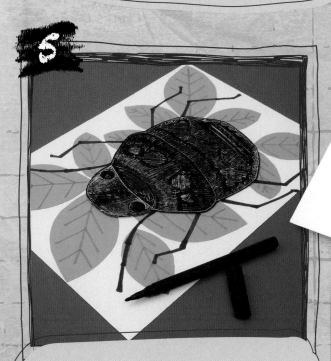

Cut your bug out and glue it onto the leafy background. Draw the legs and the antennae on with a black marker.

JEWEL BUG FACT
Some jewel bugs are not only colorful, they even look shiny and metallic!

TERMITE MOUND

Some termites build homes, called mounds, which can be up to 30 feet (9 m) high! The mound for your crafty colony of termites can be much smaller.

1

Cut cardboard into a wavy shape. Stack your seedling pots and stick them upside down onto the shape using glue.

2

Cover everything in a layer of glue and sprinkle sand over the top. Shake off the excess sand and leave to dry.

3

Mix the sand with glue and use the mixture to build little turrets. Place them around the mound.

4

Glue one and a half pumpkin seeds together onto the sand to make the head and body of a termite. You can create a colony by adding many more.

5

Paint each termite brown. Then draw their legs onto the sand using black paint.

TERMITE FACT

A lot of termites are born blind. They spend most of their lives inside the dark mound.

BUMBLEBEES

Bumblebees look a bit like honeybees, but they are bigger and fluffier. Follow these steps to make fuzzy bumblebees using pipe cleaners!

You will need:
2 black and 2 yellow pipe cleaners
Thick plastic, such as acetate sheets
Scissors
Googly eyes
Fabric glue
Pencil
Ruler

Twist a black and a yellow pipe cleaner together at one end, so they are joined.

Start wrapping the pipe cleaners around your thumb. Finish by pulling your thumb out and pushing the ends of the pipe cleaners into the hole where your thumb was.

3

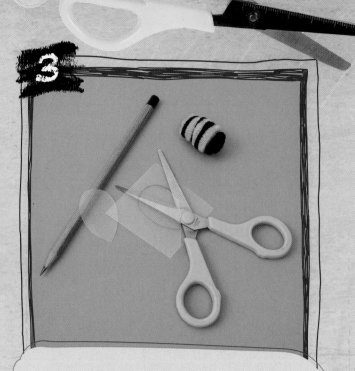

Draw 2 wing shapes on a plastic sheet and cut them out. Stick these wings to the body using fabric glue.

4

Cut 6 lengths of black pipe cleaner that are 1⅜ inches (3cm) long. Bend them into leg shapes and stick them under the body.

5

Cut 2 short pieces of yellow pipe cleaner and stick them into the head to make antennae. Glue some googly eyes onto the bumblebee's face.

BUMBLEBEE FACT
Bumblebees only make enough honey to feed their young. The honey we eat comes from honeybees.

PRAYING MANTIS

A praying mantis is hard to spot because it looks like the twigs and leaves it lives on. Make your own praying mantis to hide in plants around your home!

1

Cut 2 bendy straws to be 3⅝ inches (9cm) long. Place them onto the outside prongs of a plastic fork and bend them back.

2

Draw a face shape and eyes on green foam with a black marker. Cut out the face.

3

Tape the foam face onto the antennae. Wrap the whole fork in green electrical tape.

4

Wrap pipe cleaners around the head, middle and bottom, twisting them into place. Bend them into leg shapes to make your praying mantis stand up.

5

Cut out foam shapes for the front legs and the back of the body. Glue them in place.

PRAYING MANTIS FACT

This insect is called a praying mantis because it often folds its front legs into a praying position.

CATERPILLAR COLLAGE

You will need:

Lots of colored, patterned paper
Scissors
Glue stick
2 sheets of green card stock, 8½ by 11 inches (21.5 x 28cm)
Pencil
Black pen
Googly eyes
Compass

Caterpillars come in many different sizes and colors. Choose lots of colored, patterned paper to create your caterpillar collage!

1

Fold green card stock in half, open it up and fold each side into the middle. Open up so you have 3 folds in the card stock. Number them 1-3, from left to right.

2

Fold the left hand side so that it lines up with fold 3. Open it up again. Fold the right hand side so that it lines up with fold 1 and open it up again.

3

Fold the paper using the creases to create a "T" shape. Glue the folds into place.

4

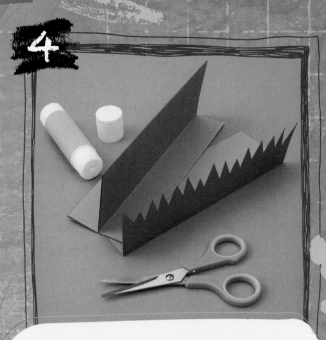

Cut the short edge of a sheet of green card stock to look like grass. Fold it and stick it to the T-shaped card stock.

5

Cut out lots of circles from colorful paper. Stick them onto the green card stock in the shape of a caterpillar. Draw its legs and mouth in black pen and stick on googly eyes. You can add 2 strips of paper to make antennae!

CATERPILLAR FACT
Did you know that caterpillars live for about a week before they start to turn into butterflies?

GLOSSARY

colony — a big group of animals that lives together

gem — a stone that is often shiny and is very precious

metallic — when something looks like metal

prey — the animal that another animal hunts for food

seal — to lock something away

sgraffito — a craft that is made by scratching away a layer of color to show other colors underneath

steel — a strong metal that is used to build skyscrapers

unique — when something is one of a kind, not like anything else

INDEX

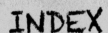
Published in 2016 by Windmill Books,
an Imprint of Rosen Publishing
29 East 21st Street, New York, NY 10010

Series editor: Julia Adams
Craft photography: Simon Pask, N1 Studios
Additional images: Shutterstock

Cataloging-in-Publication Data
Lim, Annalees.
Creepy-crawly crafts / by Annalees Lim.
p. cm. — (Creating creature crafts)
Includes index.
ISBN 978-1-5081-9101-8 (pbk.)
ISBN 978-1-5081-9102-5 (6-pack)
ISBN 978-1-5081-9103-2 (library binding)
1. Handicraft – Juvenile literature.
2. Insects in art – Juvenile literature.
I. Lim, Annalees. II. Title.
TT160.L56 2016
745.5—d23

Manufactured in the United States of America
CPSIA Compliance Information Batch #BW16PK: For Further information contact Rosen Publishing New York, New York at 1-800-237-9932